Poems I Meant to Write

Danielle Lipford

BookLeaf Publishing

India | USA | UK

Presentation by *BookLeaf Publishing*

Web: www.bookleafpub.com

E-mail: info@bookleafpub.com

ISBN: 9789360941192

First edition 2024

Poems I Meant to Write

I saw a painting that inspired me to tell a poem,
about a paintbrush,
how each new dip of paint,
altered its personality.
It was elated with each dive into yellow,
and every stroke of green,
consumed it with jealousy.
The blending of paints left it confused,
because blue made it sad and red left it mad,
but blue and red make purple
and how does one feel purple?

I passed a large fountain,
the sound flooded my brain,
conjuring images of a large river.
Deep water and rapid currents,
a river that was frigid and relentless.
The poem about the paintbrush drowned,
and a story of adventure and sacrifice
bobbed on the surface in its place.
I gripped the idea tightly,
crafted a piece that would
leave my audience in shambles.

I reached for a pen and glanced at a quarter,

deep in the bowels of my bag,
hidden beneath an empty cough drop wrapper,
resting on a phone charger with exposed wires.
Tucked away for who knows how long,
getting glances of the sun when I searched for
chapstick,
haphazardly moving things around,
unaware of the secret treasures that lie inside.
It made me wonder what else this quarter has
seen,
what it had been traded for,
if it was desperate to be spent.
I grabbed the quarter and left the river story,
stored it in the depths of my bag,
wondering how long it'll take to get
rediscovered.

On my way home,
I stopped for a snack,
giving away the newly found quarter,
wishing it well on its journey.
I returned to my home,
to the well worn chair in the corner,
illuminated by a singular lightbulb,
pens and pencils littering the ground in front of
it,
the remnants of past ideas.

I opened my notebook,

turned the page too quick.
The once crisp white page,
now smeared with blood.
There's something inspiring about
a splash of color on a once
pristine piece of paper.
I went to wash my hands,
placing down the notebook,
leaving it in a graveyard of
half formed ideas,
and poems I meant to write.

Missing Memories

Heartbreak isn't listening to sad songs on the
radio,
it's donating my favorite coat,
because it used to be yours.
Your memory clings to the fabric,
woven through the individual threads.
Despite the thick fur lining,
I'm still shivering,
and I don't think it's because of the snow.

It's finding new favorite places to go,
because the last time I went there was with you.
The blowing wind carries the echoes of your
laughter,
I still feel the weight of your hand in mine,
gripping it tightly as you point to something in
the distance.

It's not giving you a ride home,
the crash of thunder on the other side of the
door,
fluorescent flashes of lightning,
revealing just how flooded the streets are.
I can't let you into my car,

your phone still automatically connects to the
stereo,
the tether of the bluetooth,
 a reminder that
I let you back in.

It's taking myself out on dates,
buying myself fresh flowers,
telling myself compliments in the mirror.
It's realizing how easy it is to love myself the
way I wanted you to.
Heartbreak isn't not being with you,
it's realizing I settled.

Fleeting Freedom

I want to fly like Icarus
the taste of freedom on my lips,
the putrid smell of my own boiling flesh
invading my nose with each drip of melted wax.
Freedom isn't escaping,
it's laughing as your body shatters like glass
dying after touching the sun.

I want to love like Eurydice,
eyes locked with my beloved.
Icy-cold hands dragging me back
to the darkest parts of the Underworld.
Freedom isn't leaving hell,
it's locking eyes with you one last time,
knowing you came to save me.

I want to help like Prometheus,
view humanity bloom like flowers.
The feeling of my liver being gouged out of my
chest,
feeling the skin sew itself together in preparation
for tomorrow.
Freedom isn't defying the Gods,
it's aiding those in need of help,
knowing they prospered because of you.

I want to live a Greek Tragedy,
accepting that no matter my fate,
I was able to be free.

Möbius

I hope life is like a möbius strip,
destined to loop around itself,
no true end or beginning.

Living an entire life,
feeling love and heartbreak,
only to find this moment again.

If life is like a möbius strip,
all I'll have to do is keep walking,
because sooner or later,
I'll see you again.

Glass Half Empty

I don't have writer's block,
I have avoidance issues.
How do you write a poem,
without calling on your trauma?

You take some words,
string them together,
next thing you know,
you have a poem.

The problem is
gathering the words.
They're not in the dictionary,
not on some website.

They reside inside
the catacombs of my soul.
Ghosts,
waiting to be set free.

I want to let them rot,
disintegrate,
turned to ashes,
crushed to dust.

How do you bring forth emotions,
without reopening the scars on your heart?
People see your words,
but not the keyboard stained with teardrops.

I suppose I could just say,
'Man, does my heart hurt',
but those words aren't strong enough,
they don't show the suffering.

'I used your photos,
to fill the cracks in my heart'.
I drowned in my own sadness,
immortalizing you.

Rocks

People think rocks are stubborn.
Set in their ways.
Determined to never change.

Rocks are the pinnacle of adventure.
Sliding down a hill in a landslide,
trapped in an avalanche, forced down a
mountain.
Taken home by a small child,
"Mom, look at the cool rock I found!"

Rocks on the mountain
vacationed in the desert,
took a pitstop in the jungle.
They skipped across the water,
sunk on the seafloor.
Always wondering,
where they'll go next.

Sensory Overload

Sensory Overload: When your five senses -
light, sound, taste, touch, and smell- take in
more information that your brain can process.

People think sensory overload is when the lights
are too bright,
loud noises that don't go away.
They think the solution is flicking a the switch,
lying under the covers until the world calms
down.

They don't know it's the humming of the lights,
electricity has a sound and it never stops.
It's everywhere and it follows,
stabbing my brain over and over again.

It's the weight of my eyelids with every blink,
A thousand pounds everytime I open my eyes.
I'm not sure what's worse, keeping them open,
or shutting them tight.
It's the smell of fresh cooked food,
infesting my nose like rotting garbage.

It's an itch just out of reach,
a thousand bugs running on my body,

each one burrowing into me,
digging holes into my flesh.

They think its the feeling of my clothes on my
skin,
unaware that the problem is the skin itself,
constricting my bones,
trapping me within myself.

I am my own prison,
a hostage of my own making,
hoping that tomorrow,
I'll set myself free.

Strangers on a Train

She was there for me during my first heartbreak,
consoling me through the tears,
offering advice when needed,
giving jokes when the pain was too much.
I wonder if I'll ever see her again.

She was the first person to walk me to the train
station,
I was lost and alone in a new city,
scared to be trapped in a place by myself.
She showed me where to go,
ensured I got on safely,
wishing for my safe travels.
I wonder if I'll ever see her again.

We chatted in the nail salon together,
I regaled her with stories of my love life.
She sang songs of her misadventures,
We laughed until we cried,
Convinced we were kindred souls.
I wonder if I'll ever see her again.

I sometimes wonder about the people I've met,
if they're finally happy.
Do they think of me as I think of them?

I think of these strangers,
people whose life I glimpsed into,
I wonder if I'll ever see them again.

Memoriam

When you die, it's not about who holds your
hand.
The ones who stay with you as you gasp your
last breath.
Your touch, the last thing they feel,
a final tether to this world.

It's not about the last words you hear,
the melody of a long forgotten song,
melting into your ears,
the final crescendo,
playing as the story that was your life,
comes to an end.

It's about who closes your eyes,
moments after your heart has stopped pumping.
When the only thing that remains of you,
is an empty body.

The ones who tuck in your blanket,
just a little tighter,
trying to keep you warm,
even in death.

It is one thing to honor you in life,

but the one who closes your eyes,
fixes your hair,
the one who cares for you,
until you're in the ground,
scattered to the wind.
They will keep you alive,
even when you are not.

Five Million Years

18

In five million years,
I hope the stars remember,
how I loved them so.

Homesick

19

If the trees could talk,
would they say my name? Would they,
tell me to come home?

Glass Half Full

How do you edit a poem when you don't feel
those emotions anymore?
Words that are heavy with anger,
drenched with sadness.
They taste rotten on the tongue,
sound like nails on chalkboards to the ears.

They are exposed, bleeding wounds,
raw and swollen nerves,
infected gashes drowning in salt and sorrows.
Pain gushing out of each stanza,
like nuclear waste,
exploding and destroying everything around.

How do you find the words to describe your
lowest,
when you're nearly touching your wildest
dreams?
The pain that once radiated,
now an old toy left behind,
property of a life left abandoned.

How can you prevent the happiness from
peeking from your fingertips,
like a newly formed rainbow after a storm.

The colors aren't all formed yet,
but they will,
and they will be glorious.

Universal Love

I send love letters to myself across the
multiverse,
words of advice, praises and congratulations.
I tell myself my deepest secrets, my biggest
fears.
Whisper jokes to myself and hope that she
laughs.
The multiverse might not exist,
could be just a theory, wishful thinking from
scientists.
I send love letters to myself across the
multiverse,
in the odd chance that it exists,
I want the other me to know,
that she's never alone.

1:37am

You're mad because I forgot date night,
unaware that I ran out of room in my mind.

My brain is packed with things about you that
nobody will remember.

How am I supposed to remember our
anniversary
when I remember the shoes you wore to your
first job interview?

I may forget your birthday,
but I know the name of the stuffed animal you
lost years before you met me.

I don't know your favorite food,
but I remember the exact time you told me you
loved me for the first time.

I could learn your favorite song,
but I was focused on learning your favorite kind
of pen.

I don't have room for the big things,

the little things about you are much more
important.

Besides, if I don't remember,
who will?

Apprehension

I had monsters under my bed.
They're friends with the ones in my head.
I'm plagued with nightmares,
yet nobody cares.
It'll be this way 'til I'm dead.

Artistic View

My body is not a temple, it is a canvas.
Not meant to be worshiped, but admired.
I am Vincent Van Gogh's Starry Night,
 and damn do I look good.

I'm like scrap paper.
Something to doodle on, destined to always
change.
I will look different in 10 years,
covered in drawings whose meanings are no
longer relevant.

I look in the mirror and feel like I am looking,
at the Mona Lisa.
I am my favorite art museum.
My own masterpiece.

Manifestion

27

I want tear streaks on my cheeks from laughing
too hard.
I want wrinkles etched into my face in
permanent smile lines.
I want calluses on my hands, so intense a doctor
has to remove them,
each one telling a story of adventure.
I want sneakers filled with holes,
the soles a collection of dirt from around the
globe.
I want pictures of everyone I've ever met.
"Whose this man in this photograph?"
"Someone who gave me a pen at a bus stop
30,000 miles away."
I want my memories to burst at the seam.
When I'm old and gray, crippled hands and
missing teeth,
I want to close my eyes and still feel the
Jamaican sun.

The Process of Happy

Being happy after being sad is hard.
It's adjusting the way you live,
the way you see the world.

Being happy is mourning.
It's seeing how far you've fallen and
clawing your way out of the misery you're so
used to.

Being happy is exhausting.
The remains of my sadness blanket the room,
there is so much work to be done,
where do I even begin?

Being happy is scary.
The fear that something can take your good
mood,
and grind it into dust.
It's feeling the sadness you once had,
creeping in the dark,
"I was here first, you can't get rid of me."

Being happy is acceptance.
I know I'll be sad again,
but the happiness won't leave.

It rests in the back of my mind,
warming my heart.
"Just tell me when you're ready and I'll come
back."

Questions for God

If I could talk to God,
I'd ask Him about His favorite part of Heaven.
I'd ask Him if He missed Lucifer,
because he's the Devil now,
but he was His son first.
I want to know His favorite color,
how He feels about flowers.
Humanity was made in His image,
but we don't know what the image is.
How can I listen to the Bible,
it doesn't tell me God's favorite star,
it doesn't tell me if He's happy.

A Passing Moment

I am not the one to call when your sorrows are
suffocating,
killing you from the inside out.
I am not going to change your life,
or inspire you to be the best you that you can be.

I'll lend you a pen, and won't ask for it back.
I'll grab you a snack from the vending machine,
when I see your favorite chips have been
restocked.
After a rough day at work,
where your boss made you cry,
and you left your lunch at home,
I'll pick up your keys when they clatter to the
ground.

I am merely a fleeting moment,
a quick burst of joy,
long forgotten by tomorrow.
I won't change your life,
but I'll improve your day.

Mirage

I think I was a pirate in a past life.
It feels as real as the life I live now.
I cannot tell if it is a daydream,
or a memory.

I stand at the helm of a ship
A storm rages around us,
threatening to drag us to the bottom of the sea.
Lightning illuminates the sky,
my crew scurries around the deck,
lowering sails and securing cargo.
The wind howls in my ear, it's almost deafening.
A wave crashes over the ship, bone-chilling
water drenches me.
This is where I belong.
Another wave collides with the ship and -

The car jolts from the pothole littered ground.
High beams illuminate the highway.
I am stuck in a sea of traffic,
my hardened crew are stoned 20 year olds.
"Roll up the window, we're getting soaked!"
The window rolls up, I squint at my reflection.
For a brief second, a pirate squints back at me.
Another flash of high beams, and it's gone.

A joke is told,
the whole car erupts with laughter.
This is where I belong.
"Turn on the music, Danni!"
I reach for the radio, increase the volume and -

A sea shanty pours from the mouths of my crew.
We survived the storm.
The stars shine in the sky.
Drinks flow like waterfalls,
the party rages as if it were our last.
I want to stay in this moment forever.
A bottle of rum is passed to my hand,
I grip it like a lifeline, as if it were the only thing
holding me here.
"Captain, do you miss home?"
My mind fills with thoughts of forgotten jokes
and loud music.
Car lights and rolled up windows.
I close my eyes and -

I am in my first apartment.
Nine stories up,
drinking wine coolers with my roommate.
I glance out the windows,
city lights drown out the shine of the stars.
"Danni, do you miss home?"
I still smell the scent of the ocean,
can feel the water splashing me from the waves.

"Why are you crying?"
I glance around the once gray, barren walls
covered in artwork.
A movie playing on tv, homemade cookies
baking in the oven.
I could live in this moment forever.
"They're not tears, it's seawater."

9 789360 941192